THE BIG BOOK OF
MAZES

EDITED BY JEFFREY A. O'HARE

THE BIG BOOK OF

MAZES

EDITED BY JEFFREY A. O'HARE

Copyright © 2002 by Boyds Mills Press

Published by Bell Books
Boyds Mills Press, Inc.
A Highlights Company
815 Church Street
Honesdale, Pennsylvania 18431
Printed in the United States of America

U.S. Cataloging-in-Publication Data
(Library of Congress Standards)

The big book of mazes / edited by Jeffrey A. O'Hare. —1st ed.
[72] p. : col. ill. ; cm.
Summary: A collection of fabulous labyrinths from top
puzzle magazines, as well as an extensive selection of all new mazes.
ISBN 1-56397-990-X
1. Maze puzzles. 2. Logic puzzles. 3. Puzzles. I. O'Hare, Jeffrey A. II. Title.
793.738 21 2002   AC CIP

First edition, 2002
Book designed by Randy Llewellyn
The text of this book is set in 12-point New Century Schoolbook.
Visit our Web site at www.boydsmillspress.com

10 9 8 7 6 5 4 3 2 1

Cover illustration by Arieh Zeldich

At the Vet's

Wally Waxwing is a vexed vet. He's been an animal doctor long enough
to know when a woodpecker is about to get out and into trouble.
Help Wally weave his way through walruses and wallabies
to weach—er, reach that
woodpecker.

Answer on page 66

Ice Breaker

Each of these skaters is displaying some fancy footwork. But one of them had a head start. See if you can follow the trails and discover which slippery skater didn't start from the line.

Illustrated by Lynn Adams

START

4

Stan

Eddie

Hedy

Ann

Neddy

Fran

Answer on page 66

Cookie Cutups

Work your way around the tray to find out who gets the most cookies.

Illustrated by Arieh Zeldich

Answer on page 66

Alphabeads

Start at the top with *A*. Move up, down, left, right, or diagonally to the nearest *B*. From there, move to the nearest *C*. Connect the beads to make an alphabet necklace from *A* to *Z*.

START

D	A	L	W	F	J	K
K	N	B	R	D	I	O
M	C	D	K	F	G	A
P	I	R	E	B	H	X
R	S	J	X	M	K	I
F	H	F	O	T	J	O
M	O	Q	R	V	K	T
A	X	G	Q	L	B	K
F	T	M	F	W	M	P
U	O	D	N	X	F	N
V	M	B	R	S	O	L
R	I	X	S	Q	P	X
S	W	T	X	P	F	P
M	S	X	U	S	O	A
K	Y	V	S	N	U	G
R	V	W	J	X	D	M
T	N	X	W	I	I	J
M	Y	P	K	N	F	S
Z	M	T	L	R	B	E

FINISH

Answer on page 66

7

Tower Steps

This group is "cow-nting" on you to help them find the path to the tower.

START

FINISH

Answer on page 66

Illustrated by Lynn Adams

9

The Circle of Serpents

Professor Periwinkle and his friends are trying to reach the sacred Circle of Serpents. You may be able to find the right route, but be careful! Numerous jungle creatures are lurking along the way. How many can you spot?

START

Illustrated by Charles Jordan

Answer on page 66

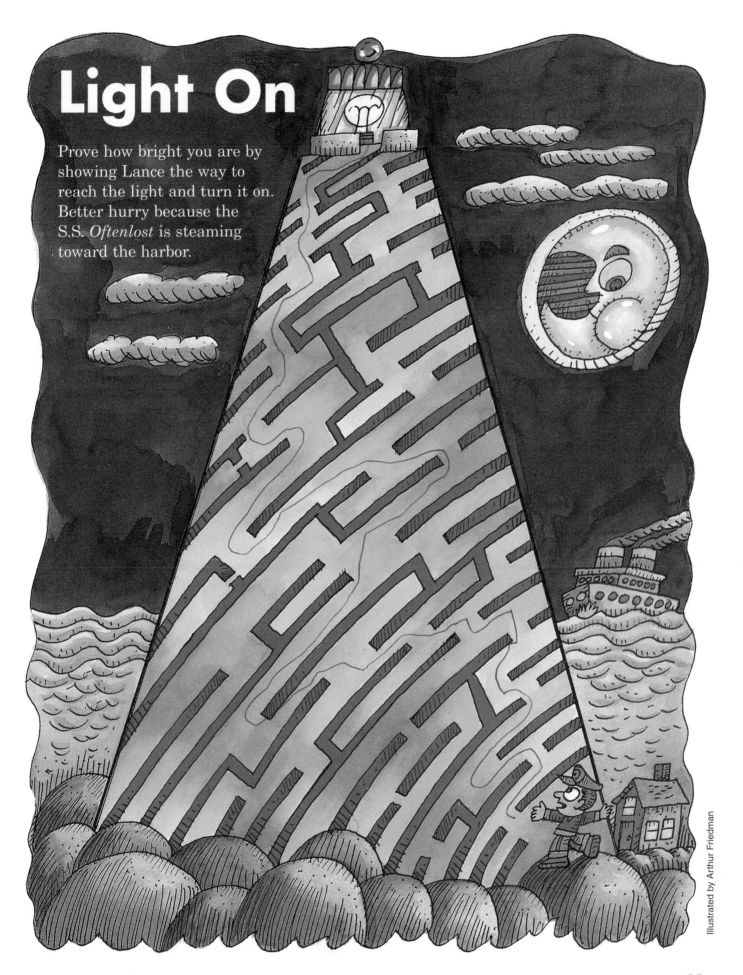

Light On

Prove how bright you are by showing Lance the way to reach the light and turn it on. Better hurry because the S.S. *Oftenlost* is steaming toward the harbor.

Illustrated by Arthur Friedman

Answer on page 67

The Wild West

During their last robbery, the Dalton gang accidentally dropped a set of pictures that showed the way to their hideout. Now Sheriff Sam is hot on their trail. The problem is that the pictures are all out of order. If you figure out in which order the pictures belong, you'll help the sheriff corral those outlaws. Hint: Sam knows that *A* is the first photo on the trail.

E

F

G

H

I

J

K

L

Illustrated by Jon Davis

START

Illustrated by Marc Nadel

FOR B.
LETTUCE
♥ mom

Rabbit Garden

Bungee Bunny's mom
dropped her a line with a
lot of lettuce. If you help
her find it, Bungee will
really jump for joy.

14

Answer on page 67

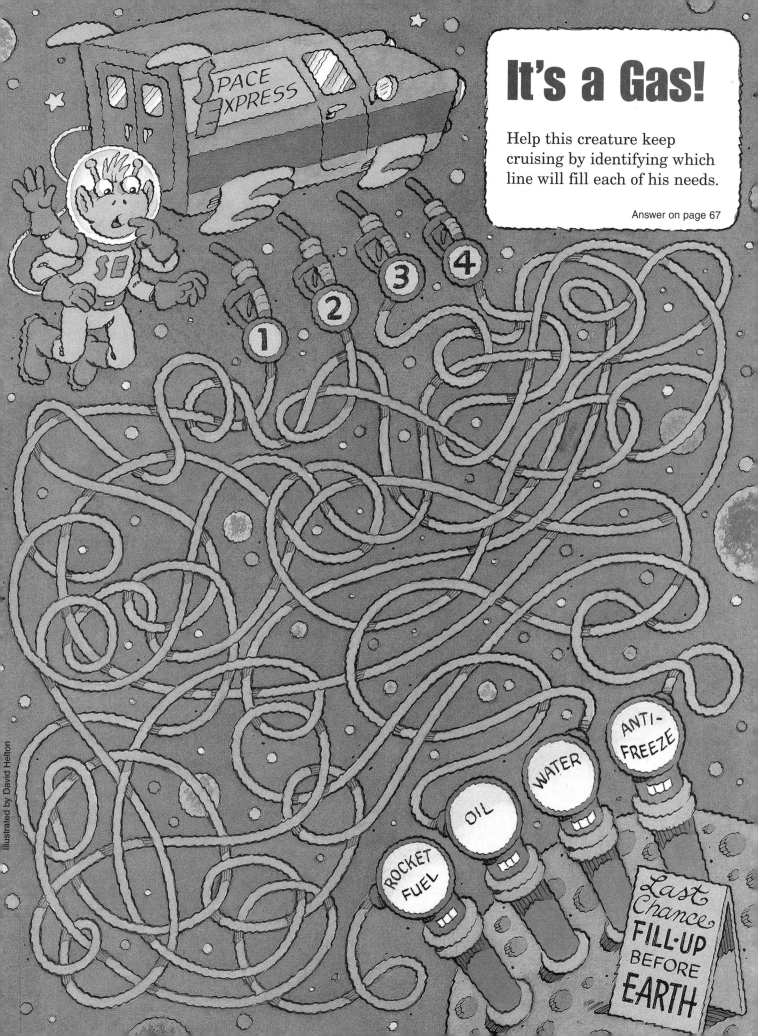

It's a Gas!

Help this creature keep cruising by identifying which line will fill each of his needs.

Answer on page 67

Uneasy Riders

Two matching riders are in this race. Find the path that will let one twin cycle to the other. You can ride only within the pack, not around the outside.

Bow-Wow Boaters

Follow the ropes to match each "hot dog" skier to the barking boaters.

Answer on page 67   Illustrated by R. Michael Palan

Grouchy Tiger, Hidden Dragon

This fuzzy feline is getting frustrated trying to find his fire-breathing friend.
Can you solve this hide-and-seek by showing Tyrone the one true path to Darryl?

Illustrated by Marc Nadel

FINISH

Answer on page 67

Wild Gift Chase

A gift is waiting for you at the Lazy Daisy Ranch. Follow the directions and collect letters from the map to find your treasure. Write the letters in the matching numbered spaces below.

A S U R P R I S E
6 7 2 8 1 8 5 7 3

P A R T Y
1 6 8 4 9

ENTRANCE

1. Trot over to the stable for letter number one.

2. The second letter is in with the pigs.

3. Fly over to the birdhouse for the third letter.

4. Look in the well for your fourth letter.

5. The doghouse has letter number five.

6. Go back to the ranch entrance for the sixth letter.

7. Find letter seven at the swimming hole.

8. Letter eight is crowing atop the chicken coop.

9. The final letter—and your gift—is at the barn.

Illustrated by Judith Hunt

Answer on page 67

Building-Brick Breakdown

Buddy's plastic-brick skyscraper completely collapsed when a bulldozer crashed into the main entrance. Follow the bricks to find the one path that leads to the toy container.

BOATLOAD O' BRIKKOS

Illustrated by Marc Nadel

Answer on page 67

Power Surge

This RV Robot is almost M.T. It will take all its power to avoid
the black hole while picking up both batteries before heading to
the charger. Will you accept this mission?

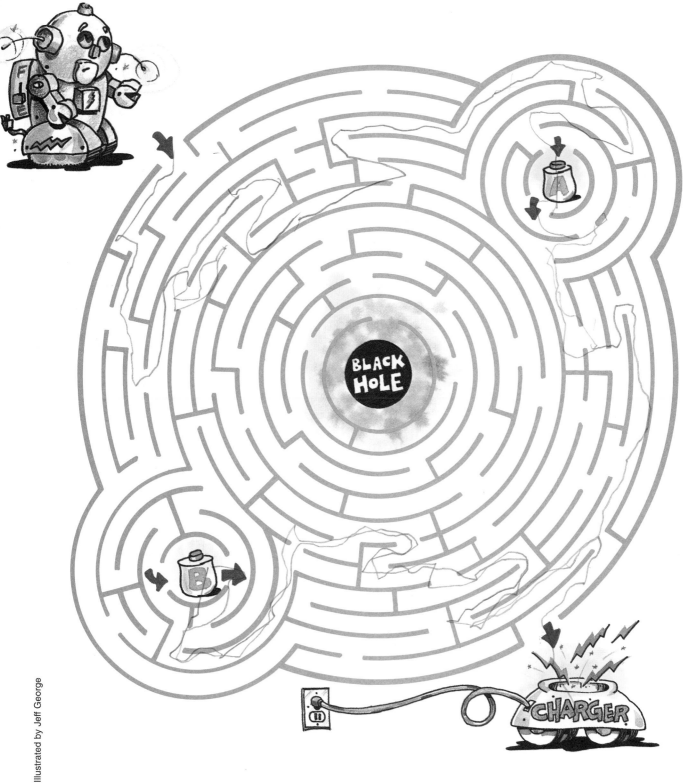

Answer on page 68

Train of Thought

All aboard the Tiny Town Train. To find out what cargo the train is carrying, you'll need to read the letters along the right route. Show the train how to reach the finish line, and then read all the letters you've crossed over. If you do it right, you should uncover the cargo.

To help you keep track of the treasure, write your letters in these blanks.

___ ___ ___ ___ ___ ___ ___

ELLICOTT CITY

START

Illustrated by Marc Nadel

Treasure Trail

Follow the glittering words on the treasure map from START to END. The words may read forward, backward, up, or down, but not diagonally. The words will appear more than once, and they may appear in any order. However, they do form one connected line from the START.

**DIAMOND GOLD OPAL TOPAZ
SILVER EMERALD RUBY**

```
          D I A M O N D I A M O N
START →   G O L D S I L D R D R D
          E L D T O P V L U L U R
          M Z L B Y A E A B O B U
          E A O R U Z O P Y G Y B
          R P G S I L V E R I S Y
          A O G O L E R E V L G O
          L T D I A M O N D L D S
          D L O G Y E R A L D G O
          E M E R A L D L O G D L
          V L A P O R E V L I S D
          E R L I S D L A R E M E
          R U B Y T O P A G O L D
          T O P A Z O P Z A L E M
                      ↓
                     END
```

Answer on page 68

26

Route to the Ring

Find the path that will get Rock Rogan to the ring in time for his big match with Steamroller Smith.

Illustrated by Charles Jordan

Answer on page 68

Spider Web

Answer on page 68

Help Fretful Fly exit the web before Spider gets back.

Track the Trucks

Each of these five trucks is loaded with one hundred boxes of shoes. Each circle represents a delivery stop along the route. How many boxes of shoes will each truck have left to deliver to the shoe stores at the end of the routes?

SHOE WAREHOUSE

1 2 3 4 5

22 14 11

2 32 18

16 28

4

21 33

6 12

20

4

40 12 5 20

SID'S SNEAKERS

12 4

80

30 3

16 14

2

PENNY'S PUMPS

SHERRY'S SHOES

Answer on page 68

LARRY'S LOAFERS

HELEN'S HEELS

Illustrated by Allan Eitzen

Pond Ponder

Fritzi Frog was on the far side of the pond when it began to rain. Now there are triple ripples on the water. Help Fritzi find a way to wade through the surging circles.

Answer on page 68

START

Illustrated by Marc Nadel

FINISH

Trail Mix

Howdy, partner. Welcome to New Mexico. Can you find the trail from Fort Union to Santa Fe?

Have you found the correct trail? As you traced the path, you crossed over some letters. Write them in order in these spaces to find the name of New Mexico's state gem:

__ __ __ __ __ __ __ __ __ __ __ __

Answer on page 69

Illustrated by Frank Bolle

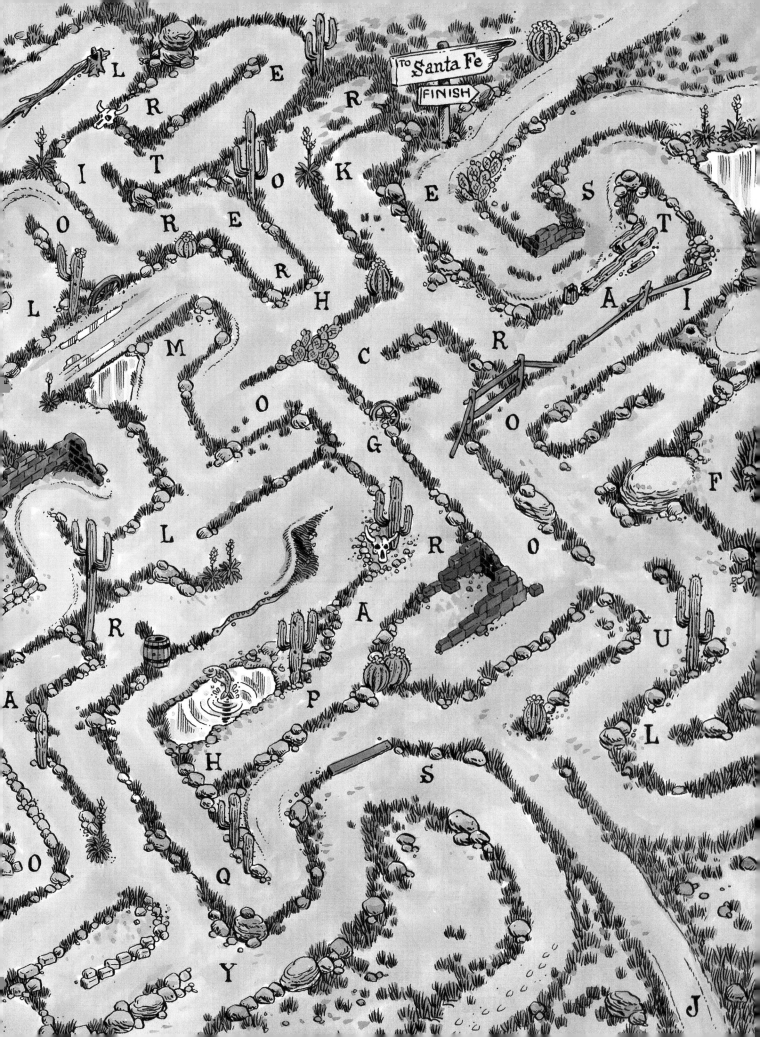

One Up

Marty Megabyte is a mathematical master. But he isn't too magnificent at mazes. Help him work his way through this maze by going up only one number in each sum. For example: 0+1=1. From there, move to 1+1, which equals 2. Next, look for a block that equals 3, and so on. Look up, down, across, backward, or diagonally. Hints: The sums will only increase, not decrease. The correct path has fifteen steps between IN and OUT.

10 x 0	3 x 3 − 2	12 − 2 + 1	3 x 4	5 x 3 − 2
16 − 6	11 + 3 − 7	1 + 2 + 3 + 4	20 + 4 ÷ 6	2 + 3 + 4 + 5
18 ÷ 2 − 88	4 x 2 ÷ 3	0 x 11	10 − 5 + 4	15 x 1 → OUT
12 − 2 ÷ 5	6 x 1 x 2	4 x 2 ÷ 8	4 x 2	17 − 7 ÷ 5
8 − 4 + 1	3 + 2 + 1	9 − 2	18 ÷ 9	10 − 4
9 ÷ 3	10 ÷ 2	7 − 7	1 + 2 + 3	3 x 3
7 − 6 + 1	2 + 2	5 − 3	8 ÷ 4	1 + 4
4 − 3	1 x 0	3 x 1	6 − 5	2 ÷ 2
IN → 0 + 1	1 + 1	2 ÷ 0	3 x 0	10 − 8

Answer on page 69

Illustrated by John Bennett

Proud Portrait

Terence is trying to clean his pop's portrait. But the timid tiger is too shy to give that spider the brush-off. Help the spider find a path from the nose back up to the spider web in time for Terence to finish cleaning. The spider won't cross over any lines on either the portrait or frame.

Illustrated by Arieh Zeldich

Answer on page 69

Garden Maze

While on vacation, you find this lovely garden maze. You've been lost in it for hours. Now you need to figure out how to get out. Find the one path that leads back to your hotel.

Answer on page 69

Illustrated by Marc Nadel

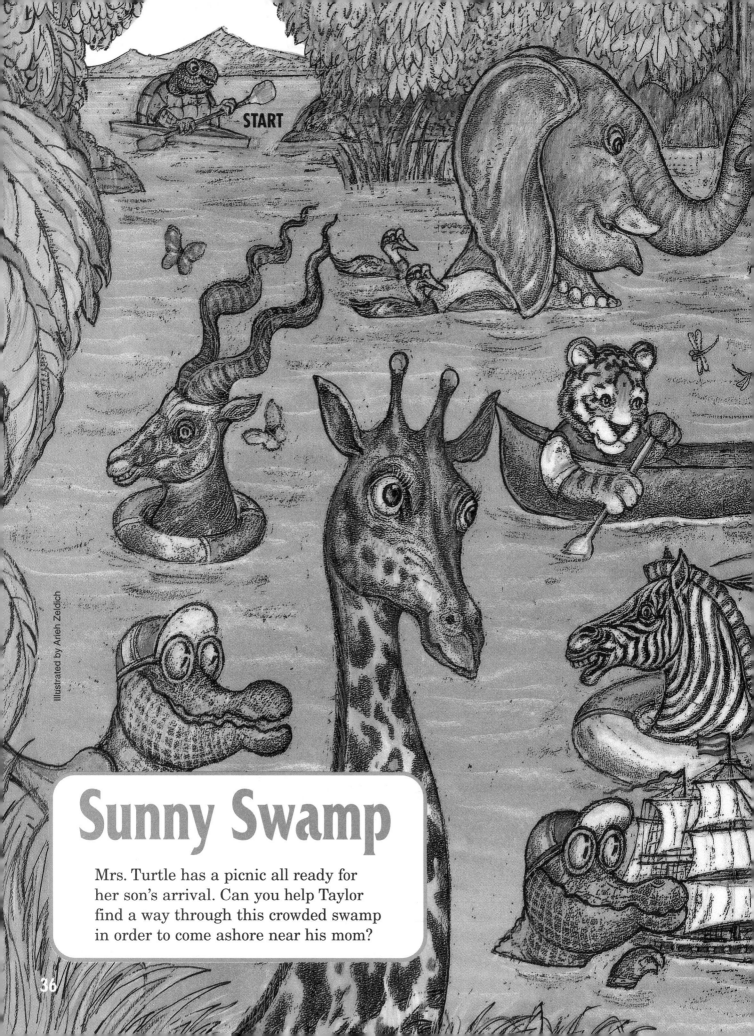

START

Sunny Swamp

Mrs. Turtle has a picnic all ready for her son's arrival. Can you help Taylor find a way through this crowded swamp in order to come ashore near his mom?

Illustrated by Arieh Zeldich

Answer on page 69

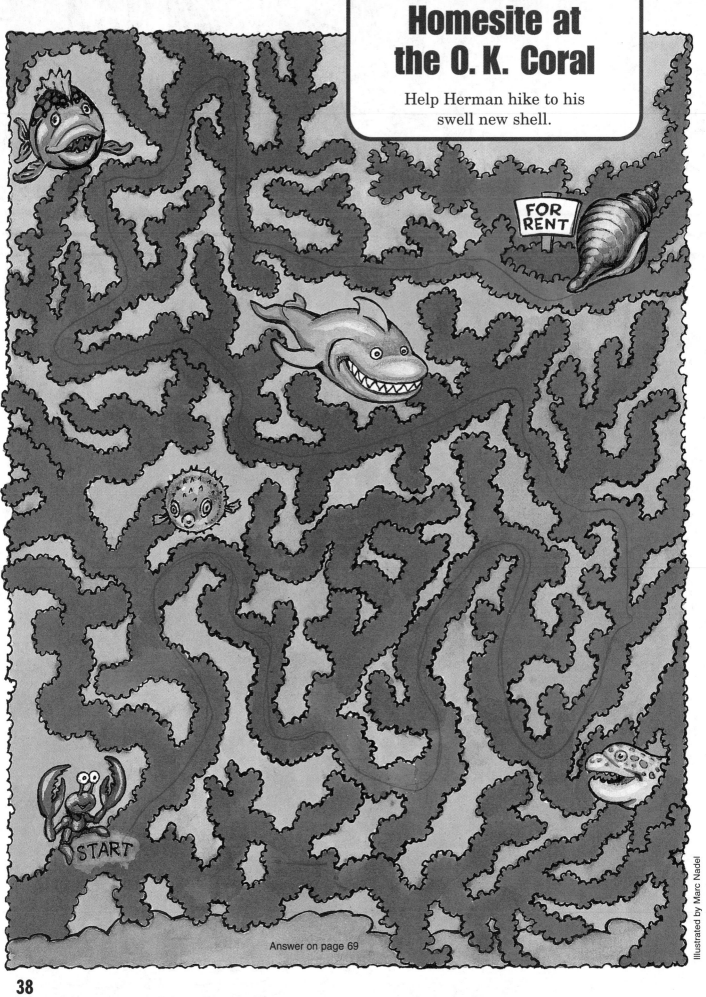

Homesite at the O. K. Coral

Help Herman hike to his swell new shell.

FOR RENT

START

Answer on page 69

Illustrated by Marc Nadel

Year of the Dragons

You will be fortunate indeed if you can tell what color each numbered dragon is about to be painted. Track back along the scales to go from each number to the tail.

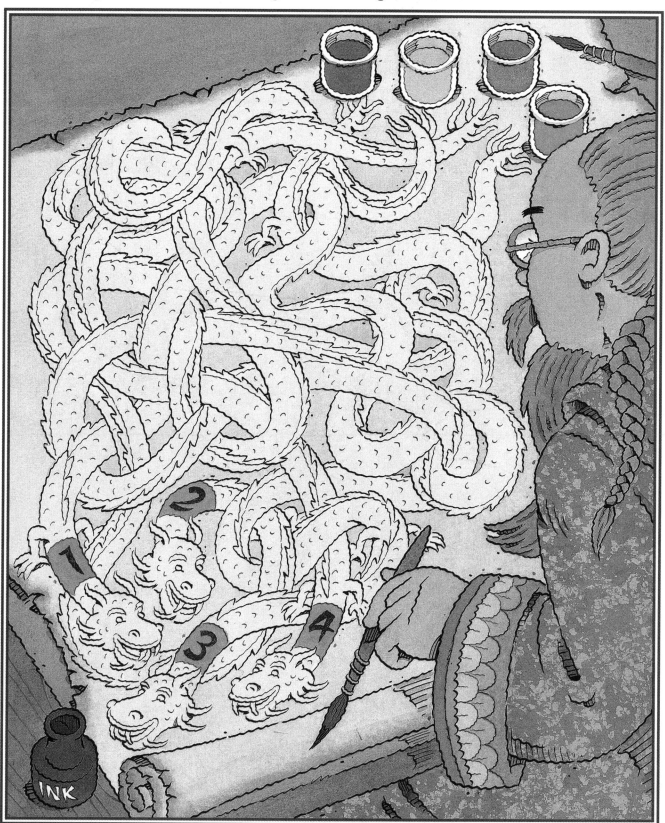

Answer on page 69

Cave at Emptor

You should have been more careful when you bought your ticket for this ride. Now you're stuck between the stalagmites of Emptor Cave. You can see the exit, but can you find your way there?

Illustrated by Lynn Adams

Answer on page 70

Octopuzzle

Which of Otto's tentacles has snared the strawberry seaweed soda?

Illustrated by Marc Nadel

Answer on page 70

Bath Time

Doris needs to dunk with Dolores. Everything will be just ducky if you can find a way for her to go through the bubbles without popping any before she reaches the bathtub.

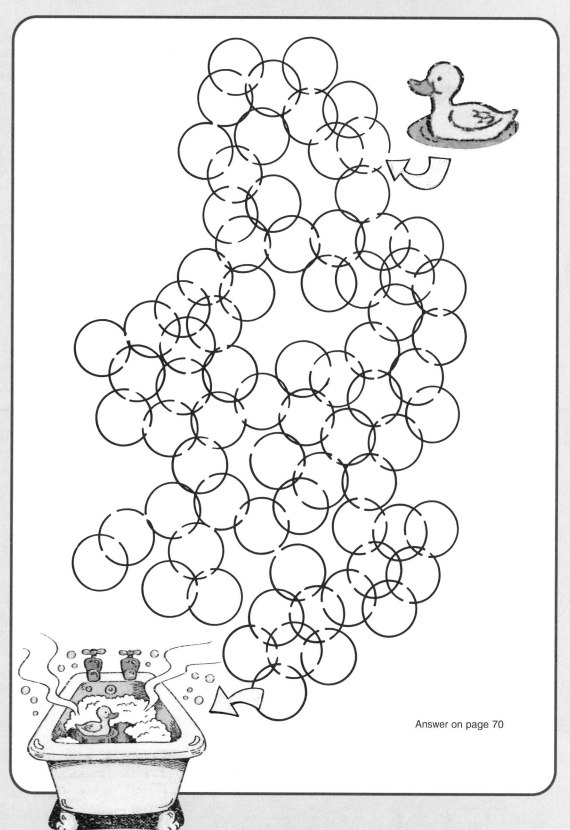

Answer on page 70

Theme Parking

It's sure no amusement to look for a place to park. Drive carefully as you try to move your car from START to FINISH.

Answer on page 70

Illustrated by Frank Bolle

START

Root Route

Truffle hunters Trevor and Troy are tracking down the world's tastiest treat, the Trupnik Truffle. Trace the trail that will make them triumphant.

START

Illustrated by Marc Nadel

Answer on page 70

Minus Maze

To find your way through this maze, subtract the first pair of numbers (6-1). Draw a line to the answer (5), then move to the next pair of numbers and do the same. Answers may be to the left, right, up, or down.

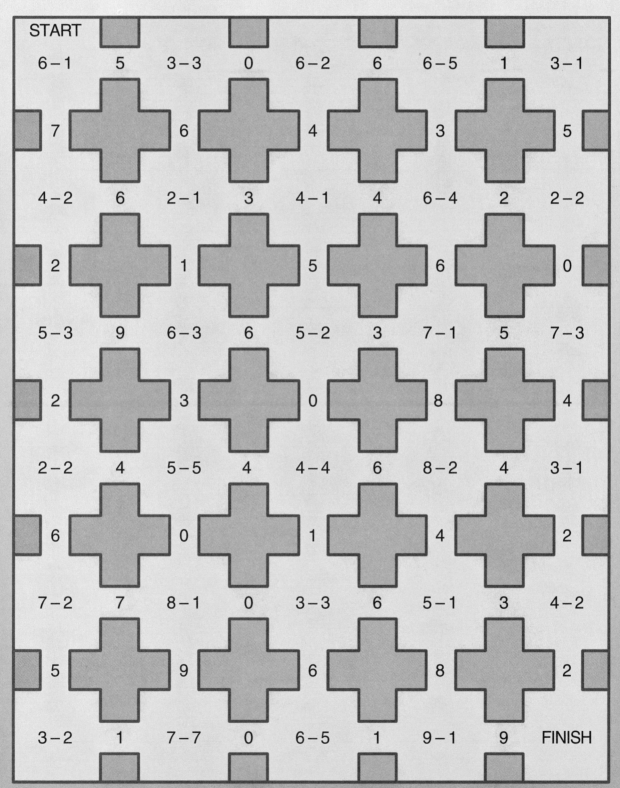

Pumped Up

Help Percy plow the path to his plump prize pumpkin.

Illustrated by Marc Nadel

Answer on page 70

Don't Be Chicken

Find the path through the ladders and open doorways that will lead Mrs. Little to Junior.

Illustrated by Arthur Friedman

Answer on page 71

Got Lost

Phil and Francine need to get back to
their friends. See if you can spot the path
that will lead them back from the rock
carvings to the Anasazi houses.

Answer on page 71

Illustrated by Ron Zalme

51

Castle Crawl

Isn't this one sandy, dandy castle? No one will be crabby if you help Clyde crawl his way through from START to FINISH.

FINISH

START

Illustrated by Rob Sepanak

Answer on page 71

Vavoom Video Game

How many stars can Cuscus collect on the most direct route home to the Big Tree? Watch out for the members of the Tickling Trio, who are also seeing stars.

Illustrated by Marc Nadel

Answer on page 71

Take a Peak!

These hardy climbers are working their way through the White Mountains of New Hampshire. Unfortunately, not everyone will make it to the top of this next peak. Follow the trails to see who will be the top contenders.

Will

Jill

Phil

Lil

Answer on page 71

Rug Run

Run this robot mouse through the rug
to the hole without crossing any lines.

FINISH

START

Illustrated by Jeff George

Answer on page 71

Magic Spell

A miller's daughter is spinning straw into gold, thanks to the secret help of a mystical little man. Now she has to guess his name, or he'll tell the king the truth. If she looks carefully, she'll see the name woven into a path leading from the spinning wheel to him. Can you spell it out for her?

START

FINISH

Illustrated by Marc Nadel

Answer on page 72

Sunken Snapshots

While scuba diving in the South Seas, Sarah snapped some shots of her magnificent underwater adventure. But now she can't remember how the pictures go together. Can you figure out which order they go in so Sarah can remember her trip? Hint: *C* is the first photo in the trail.

Answer on page 72

Illustrated by Judith Hunt

Tangled Tails

The winds have tangled these kites. Can you find who's holding which kite?

Adam

Beth

Cal

Illustrated by Judith Hunt

Answer on page 72

BATS

Boris badly wants to beat his brothers to the belfry. You can help him fly right by showing him what path to stake out.

Illustrated by Arthur Friedman

Hat Match

We'll take our hats off to you if you can find a path that connects the two matching hats without crossing any of the ribbons or going outside the display.

Illustrated by Paul Richer

Answer on page 72

Leafing Home

Which path of falling leaves
should Chipper follow to
bring his acorn safely
home to Mom?

Illustrated by Marc Nadel

FINISH

Answer on page 72

Fancy Fins

Don't bust any bubbles or cross any lines as you swim through these fishy friends to find a path to the treasure.

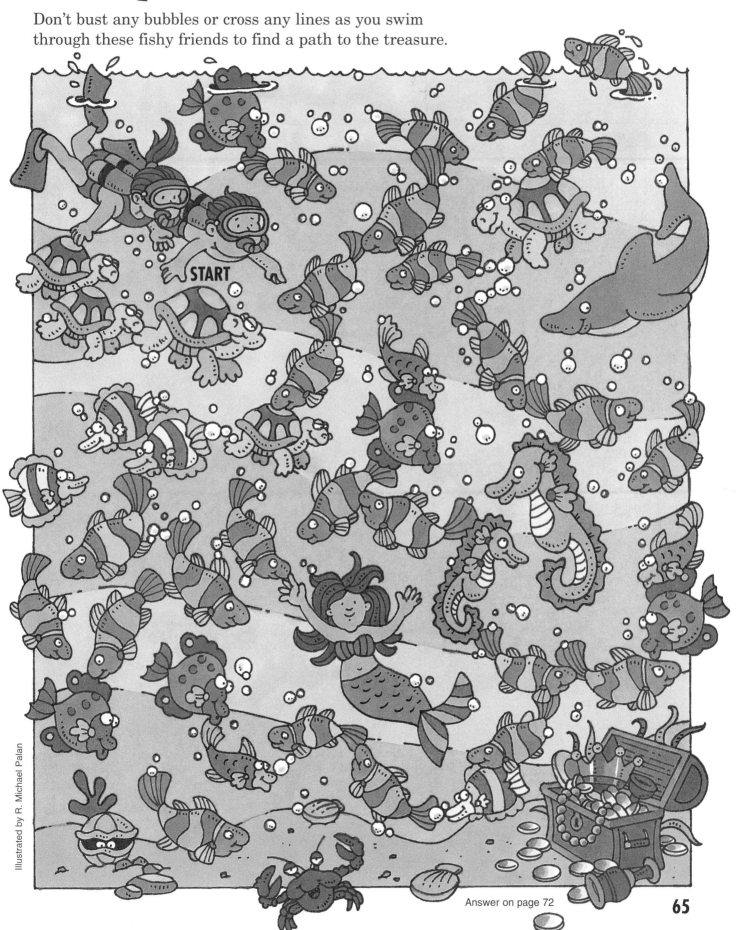

Illustrated by R. Michael Palan

Answer on page 72

Answers

Cover Lettuce Have Some

Page 3 At the Vet's

Pages 4-5 Ice Breaker
Eddie didn't start at the line.

Page 6 Cookie Cutups
Stars - 22
Circles - 21
Hexagons - 18

Page 7 Alphabeads

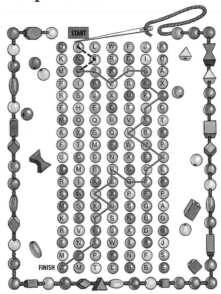

Pages 8-9 Tower Steps

Page 10 The Circle of Serpents

Page 11 Light On

Pages 12-13 The Wild West
A-E-D-H-B-F-C-L-G-J-I-K

Page 14 Rabbit Garden

Page 15 It's a Gas!

1 - Antifreeze   2 - Water
3 - Rocket fuel   4 - Oil

Pages 16-17 Uneasy Riders

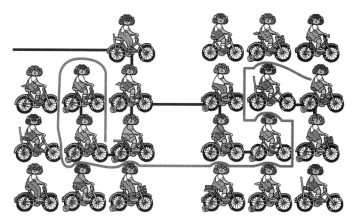

Page 18 Bow-Wow Boaters

1 - C
2 - A
3 - D
4 - B

Page 19 Grouchy Tiger, Hidden Dragon

Pages 20-21 Wild Gift Chase
A SURPRISE PARTY

Page 22 Building-Brick Breakdown

Page 23   Power Surge

Pages 24-25   Train of Thought
Treasure: Bagels

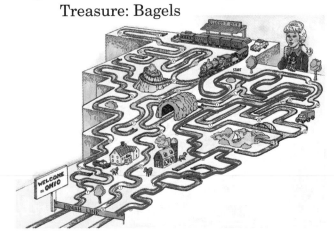

Page 26   Treasure Trail

Page 27   Route to the Ring

Page 28   Spider Web

Page 28   Track the Trucks

Trucks 1 and 5 will each have
   one box of shoes left.
Truck 2 will have fourteen boxes left.
Truck 3 won't have any boxes left.
Truck 4 will have three boxes left.

Page 29   Pond Ponder

Pages 30-31 Trail Mix
Gem: Turquoise

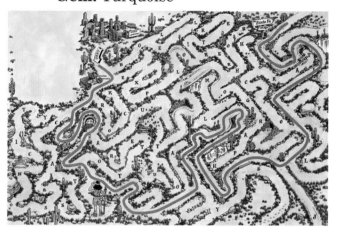

Page 32 One Up

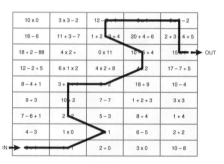

Page 33 Proud Portrait

Pages 34-35 Garden Maze

Pages 36-37 Sunny Swamp

Page 38 Homesite at the O. K. Coral

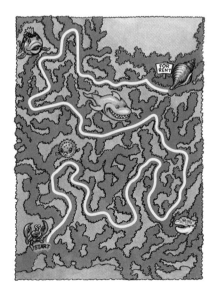

Page 39 Year of the Dragons

1- Green   3- Red
2- Blue   4- Yellow

Pages 40-41 Cave at Emptor

Page 42 Octopuzzle 2

Page 43 Bath Time

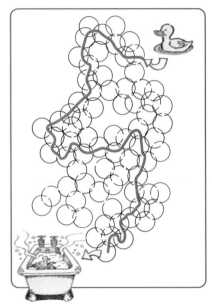

Pages 44-45 Theme Parking

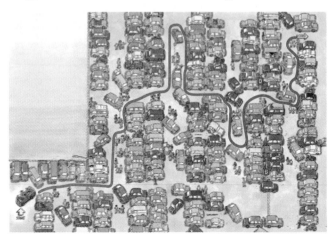

Page 46 Root Route

Page 47 Minus Maze

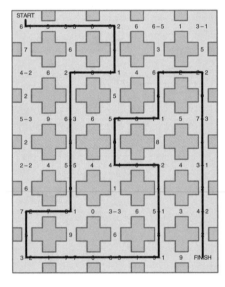

Page 48 Pumped Up

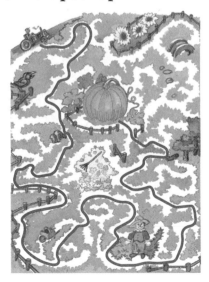

Page 49 Don't Be Chicken

Page 53 Vavoom Video Game
Seven stars

Pages 50-51 Got Lost

Pages 54-55 Take a Peak!
Will, Jill, and Lil will make it to the top.

Page 52 Castle Crawl

Page 56 Rug Run

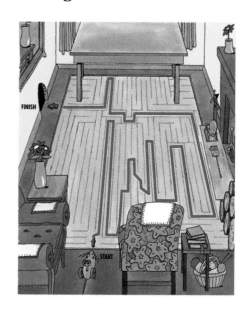

Page 57 Magic Spell

Pages 58-59 Sunken Snapshots
C-K-I-A-L-B-F-E-G-H-D-J

Page 60 Tangled Tails
Adam - butterfly
Beth - fish
Cal - diamond

Page 61 Bats

Pages 62-63 Hat Match

Page 64 Leafing Home

Page 65 Fancy Fins

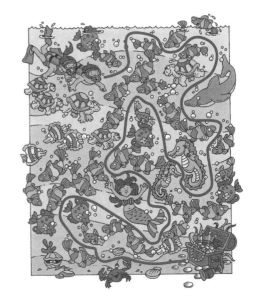